Stegosaurus

Written by Angela Sheehan
Illustrated by John Francis

Library of Congress Cataloging in Publication Data

Sheehan, Angela.
  Stegosaurus.

  Includes index.
  SUMMARY: Follows a stegosaurus through two busy days as he copes with other dinosaurs, mates, and joins a new herd.
    1. Stegosaurus—Juvenile literature.   [1. Stegosaurus.
2. Dinosaurs]   I. Francis, John, 1942-   .   II. Title.
QE862.D5S45   1981   567.9'7   81-108
ISBN 0-86592-112-1
(0-8167-1302-2 trade ed.)

Watermill Press
Mahwah, New Jersey

Brontosaurus
(Apatosaurus)

Pteranodon

Dimetrodon

Cetiosaurus

Iguanodon

Stegosaurus

Stegosaurus

Tyrannosaurus

Triceratops

Parasaurolophus

Ornithomimus

Ankylosaurus

Despite his great size, Stegosaurus just could not get rid of the creature snapping round his feet. As fast as he turned, so the sharp-toothed little dinosaur ran round him, leaping and yapping at his sides. Stegosaurus was normally more than a match for Ornitholestes but he was now too tired to run or fight. The day had been long and hot, and he and his herd had walked a long way.

As the little dinosaur grew more excited, it began to take less and less care. At last it rushed towards Stegosaurus's back legs, and the great reptile took his chance. He swung his spiked tail and Ornitholestes fell to the ground, stunned and wounded. Stegosaurus plodded away.

The last glimmer of red was fading from the sky. Stegosaurus was so far behind his herd that he could hardly make out the animals' shapes against the trees ahead. By the time he reached the forest it was dark and he could see only shadows. But he could hear strange noises. He walked a little way, trying hard to stay awake. But he was too tired. Slowly his eyes closed and he sank into a deep sleep. All night the woods rang with howls, squawks and bellowing.

When Stegosaurus woke in the morning, the birds were already singing and the forest floor was speckled with light. He raised his head to look about, when suddenly the tree next to him shook and shuddered, and the bellowing noise he had heard at nightfall boomed out again. An Archaeopteryx squawked and flapped out of the swaying tree. Stegosaurus backed away as a huge gray shape loomed up before him.

7

Now he could see where the bellowing came from. The shape was a Brontosaurus. There was a whole herd of the giants marching through the swaying trees. Stegosaurus watched as they ripped the curving fronds from high on the trunks. He looked for his own herd but they were nowhere to be seen. So he followed the giants, staying just far enough behind not to disturb them.

Stegosaurus cropped the fronds on the forest floor, while the brontosaurs stretched their long necks to reach the topmost branches. After some time the herd stopped feeding and trundled out of the forest. Stegosaurus, close behind them, blinked in the bright sunshine and felt its warmth on his back. He marched quickly after the herd, away from the damp gloom of the woods.

Soon they reached a small waterhole. The brontosaurs waddled into the water, which was just deep enough to cover and cool their backs. Stegosaurus stayed on the bank and ate the thick ferns as the giants wallowed and bellowed. The ferns were hot and steaming in the fierce midday sun, and so high that Stegosaurus was completely hidden by them.

Suddenly he heard silence and then a rumble. Peering through the greenery, he saw the brontosaur herd clambering up the slippery bank of the pool. Only one animal could not keep up with the others as they galloped away. It was an old male. Behind him sped Megalosaurus, his great mouth gaping. The hungry reptile closed on the Brontosaurus and leapt on his back. But the old dinosaur's hide was too hard for Megalosaurus to grip and he lost his balance. As he fell, the Brontosaurus lashed out with his tail and left the attacker stunned.

Stegosaurus stayed well behind his screen of ferns until the dreadful creature had gone. Now all was quiet, but Stegosaurus was all alone. There were no other creatures to warn him of danger and none to hide or run with if danger came again. So he made his way back to the woods. It was cool beneath the trees, and there were many hiding places. He kept near to the edge of the wood, moving slowly and silently. The ground rose and the forest grew thicker.

All at once, Stegosaurus came to a break in the trees. He heard the sound of rushing water, and there in front of him was a waterfall. The water tumbled down a steep slope, splashed on the rocks below, and babbled noisily away. Stegosaurus drank from the cool stream and then followed its course.

After a time, the stream widened and the fish-filled water began to flow more gently. Stegosaurus rested for a while and then went on. He had not gone far when he heard a sound he knew well. It was the call of a female Stegosaurus ready to mate. He could not see her, so he headed for the clump of bushes from which the noise had come. As he neared them, he caught sight of the female and quickened his pace. But just as he reached her, another male Stegosaurus came roaring towards him.

The animal stopped a few paces away and growled fiercely. Stegosaurus saw that his rival was old: two of the spikes on his tail were broken, and his hide was pitted with the scars of old wounds. Stegosaurus wanted the female for himself. So he challenged the old male, by growling back at him and charging at him.

The old male charged too, but he was no
match for the younger Stegosaurus. After a short fight,
the old animal lumbered away, slowly but unhurt.
Stegosaurus approached the female.

He walked towards her, turning his head from side to side and swinging his tail. She growled a warning to keep away. But he took no notice. Instead he walked slowly round and round her, still swishing his tail. After a while, she stopped growling and let him come even closer. Then she allowed him to mate with her.

The two animals stayed by the river until the evening sun began to color the cliffs and the shadows of the cycads grew longer. Soon, the insects that had hovered and darted all day over the river were gone. It was almost night.

The female Stegosaurus listened to the sound of her herd calling as they lumbered off to rest. Then she and her new mate set off to join them. Stegosaurus would once again have other animals to travel with. And his mate would soon lay her eggs.

Stegosaurus and the Jurassic World

Length (from nose to tail): 20 feet or more
Height (to top of plates): 16 feet
Weight: up to 1.8 tons

Bony plates
perhaps
used for
defense or for
temperature
control

Small head
with weak teeth

Spiky tail
used for
defense

Five toes

Three toes

The skeleton of Stegosaurus compared in size with a man

When Stegosaurus Lived

The Age of Dinosaurs is divided into three periods: the Triassic, Jurassic and Cretaceous. Stegosaurus lived during the Jurassic, about 150 million years ago.

What Stegosaurus Ate

We know from Stegosaurus's teeth that it was a plant-eater. (Meat-eaters have sharp tearing teeth, while plant-eaters have flatter teeth for grinding up tough leaves and stems.) Stegosaurus had a very small mouth with weak little teeth. So it must have spent a very great deal of its time feeding, in order to get enough nourishment for its great body. With such a short neck, too, Stegosaurus could have fed only on plants that grew low on the ground. These plants would have been mostly ferns and horsetails; there were almost no flowering plants during Jurassic times.

Enough for all

Stegosaurus did not have to share the low-growing plants with many other animals. Brontosaurus (see page 9) and the other tall plant-eating dinosaurs fed on tall plants, such as cycads (palm-like trees), maidenhair trees and conifers. Medium sized dinosaurs, such as Camptosaurus, fed on the lower branches of these trees. They stood on their hind legs to reach them. If you look at the animals that live today on the African plains, you will see the same thing. Giraffes, with their long necks, browse on the tree-tops; gerenuks rear up on their hind legs to reach the lower branches; the other antelopes feed on the bushes and grass.

"Mini" Brain in a Monster Body

Stegosaurus must have been a very unintelligent animal. For, despite a huge body, it had a brain no bigger than a walnut. People once thought that Stegosaurus had two brains: there is a large swelling in its spine which seemed to be a brain. But this second "brain" was nothing like a real one. It was merely a mass of large nerves that Stegosaurus needed to control its huge back legs and tail.

A Deadly Weapon

With fierce meat-eaters roaming the land, plant-eaters needed sturdy weapons and armor to protect themselves. Stegosaurus's spiky tail was an excellent weapon. It could easily cripple a small meat-eater, such as Ornitholestes (see page 4). This "nuisance" probably hung around the stegosaurs waiting to snap up lizards and other small creatures stirred up by their huge feet. A blow from the tail could probably also have wounded a smallish meat-eater, such as Megalosaurus (see page 12), though bigger ones would not have been kept at bay for long.

Armor or Heating?

The double row of great bony plates along Stegosaurus's back looks very fierce indeed. Any attacker that attempted to strike Stegosaurus on the back would have had a dangerous and difficult time. But, since the plates did not protect the sides or legs at all, few animals would have been stupid enough to go for the back. What use then were the bony plates to Stegosaurus?

Some scientists think that the plates helped Stegosaurus to control its temperature. Such a large dinosaur would have got very hot as it moved about. When we get hot, we sweat, and sweating makes us cooler. But dinosaurs probably could not sweat. They would have had to find a cool place or go for a swim to get rid of the heat—unless they had some other way of cooling themselves. Stegosaurus's plates could have served this purpose. A large flat area cools down much quicker than a bulky body. A large flat area also warms up quicker. So if Stegosaurus was cold, it could turn its side to the sun. The heat striking the plates would soon heat the blood in them, and the warm blood would then flow all around the body, making the whole animal warm.

Early Death and Safer Successors

Being able to control its temperature (if it could) does not seem to have helped Stegosaurus to survive. The stegosaurs died out early in the Cretaceous period. The reason for their disappearance was probably that their weapons and armor simply did not give enough protection against the great meat-eaters.

During the Cretaceous a new kind of dinosaur took the place of the stegosaurs. The ankylosaurs (see below) were smaller but had far stronger armor. Like Stegosaurus, they fed on the low-growing plants, but they could escape injury by dropping on their stomachs.

Picture Index

Apart from Stegosaurus, these are some of the other animals that you can see in the book:

Things To Do

Try to think of modern animals that are like the dinosaurs in this book. Brontosaurus for example, is like an elephant with a giraffe's long neck.

Nobody has ever seen a living dinosaur. So we can only guess what they looked like from their skeletons. The artist who drew the pictures in this book made Stegosaurus green and brown, but he could have been a different color, like his mate on page 17. Try drawing him the color you think he might have been.

You can make models of all the animals in the story with modeling clay. Use stiff card or sea shells for Stegosaurus's plates and pieces of spaghetti for his spikes. You can even model a whole scene, with paper plants and trees. If you make ankylosaurs, use pebbles for the knobs on their armor.

Two types of ankylosaur

Scolosaurus

Ankylosaurus